Every Minute Cour

**DATE DUE**

| | | | |
|---|---|---|---|
| | | | |
| | | | |
| | | | |
| | | | |
| | | | |
| | | | |
| | | | |
| | | | |
| | | | |
| | | | |
| | | | |
| | | | |
| | | | |
| | | | |
| | | | |
| | | | |
| | | | |
| | | | |
| | | | |
| GAYLORD | | | PRINTED IN U.S.A |

Also available in the *Classmates* series:

*Lesson Planning* – Graham Butt
*Managing Your Classroom* – Gererd Dixie
*Teacher's Guide to Protecting Children* – Janet Kay
*Tips for Trips* – Andy Leeder
*Stress Busting* – Michael Papworth
*Teaching Poetry* – Fred Sedgwick
*Running Your Tutor Group* – Ian Startup
*Involving Parents* – Julian Stern
*Marking and Assessment* – Howard Tanner and Sonia Jones

# Every Minute Counts

**Michael Papworth**

**continuum**
LONDON • NEW YORK

**Continuum**

The Tower Building
11 York Road
London SE1 7NX

15 East 26th Street
New York
NY 10010

*www.continuumbooks.com*

*British Library Cataloguing-in-Publication Data*
A catalogue record for this book is available from the British Library.

ISBN 0–8264–7070–X

Typeset by BookEns Ltd, Royston, Herts.
Printed and bound in Great Britain by Biddles Ltd, Guildford and
King's Lynn

# Contents

*Series Introduction*                                    vii

*Preface*                                                 ix

**Part One – The Time Management Mind-Set**

1   The 4 Secrets of Time                                  1

2   The 40-hour Week                                      13

**Part Two – Essential Skills**

3   Weekly Planning                                       28

4   5-minute Lesson Planning                              37

5   Marking                                               55

6   Report Writing                                        64

7   How to Handle Paperwork                               72

8   How to Run Meetings                                   77

**Part Three – Quick Tips**

Your briefcase                                            84

Clutter                                                   85

# Contents

Communication skills                88

Planning your day                   92

Your memory                         95

Relaxation                          96

*Reading List*                      99

# Series Introduction

*Dear Teacher*

Classmates is an exciting and innovative new series developed by Continuum, and is designed to help you improve your teaching, and your career.

With your huge workload both inside and outside of school, we understand that you have less and less time to read around your profession. These short, pithy guides have been designed with an accessible layout so that you don't have to wade through lots of dull, heavy text to find the information you need.

All our authors have experienced teaching first hand and have written this essential series with busy teachers in mind. Our subjects range from taking school trips (*Tips for Trips*) and dealing with parents (*Involving Parents*) to coping with the large amounts of stress in your life (*Stress Busting*) and creating more personal time for yourself (*Every Minute Counts*).

If you have practical advice that you would like to share with your fellow teachers and think you could write a book for this series then we would be delighted to hear from you.

We do hope you enjoy reading our *Classmates*. With very best wishes,

*Continuum's Education Team*

P.S. Watch out for our second batch of ten *Classmates*, to be launched in March 2004.

I humbly and respectfully dedicate this little work to the memory of my great friend and mentor, Grant Murray (1960–2002).

Grant guided me to the understanding of the power of having a clear mission. I miss him sorely.

'What really matters is not the date we were born or the date we die, but how we live the dash in between.' (Anon)

# Preface

Everybody knows that teaching has an incredibly high workload. This has been the subject of study and debate for many years.

The PricewaterhouseCoopers study (*Teacher Workload Study*, December 2001) determined that the average hours of a classroom teacher is of the order of 52 hours per week. Other studies and my own observations have shown results of the same order with 60+ hours being reported by some 15 per cent of classroom teachers.

It strikes me as bizarre that so much effort has been put in to identifying and studying the problem, yet no one has come up with anything which even approaches being a solution. The nearest is a document produced by the NUT (John Atkins and Karen D. Robinson. *Teacher Professionalism and Workload, client-side advice*, November 2001) which proposes a formula for a 38-hour week. The formula is perfectly sound, but no suggestion as to how it may be achieved is given.

This book offers a completely new and revolutionary approach to time management. It is also the only book on this topic (that I'm aware of) that is dedicated entirely to teachers. It is revolutionary in that it offers a two-pronged approach to the issues of managing time.

# Preface

The first part of the approach is that it is brain-based. Your brain is an incredibly powerful device that governs all that you do. Your bad habits and your good habits are deeply programmed into the neural fabric of your brain. Habits, as we all know, are VERY difficult to change. This is because the neural pathways that control your habits are very deeply embedded. In order to change from poor time management to good time management habits, you have to break the old ones and replace them with new, good ones. This book addresses just that issue.

The second part of the approach is that it is systems-based. Systems exist wherever you have two or more things that are interdependent. Most systems are stable; however a small change in part of a system can have a very large effect on another part. These changes are usually unwanted. One of the problems is that the changes are usually well separated in time; it is not always easy to trace back to the cause.

By studying and understanding the system, it is possible to find very small changes that have very large effects in the direction that you want. It's called leverage. When you identify the leverage points and apply just the right amount of pressure, the system changes favourably. If you then also neutralize the forces that made the system stable before and add new stabilizing components to the system, it becomes self-sustaining.

To summarize: [How typical of a teacher!]

◆ You re-program your brain to accept the good habits and override bad habits and

◆ You create a self-sustaining system to maintain the good habits.

These two approaches taken together are very powerful.

Add to that a profound understanding of exactly the issues that affect teachers that only a teacher can have and you have what is in front of you now: the perfect solution to time-management problems for teachers.

The book is divided into three sections.

The first section outlines the basic ideas of this approach to time management. These ideas are central to the entire book. It is vital to have a profound understanding of the basic ideas to create a sound foundation on which to build the techniques.

The second section addresses all the most pressing problems that teachers find in a typical working environment.

The techniques given must pass two tests:

◆ First of all, they must enable you to do an excellent job fast. There is no question of a trade-off between quality and speed. They must both be present.

◆ Secondly, they must produce educationally sound output. In every case, this has been uppermost in my mind. There is absolutely no point in doing the job unless it produces excellent education excellently delivered.

They pass both tests.

You will notice that there is a theme running throughout the entire section. The theme is that you

# Preface

need to do your thinking first and your production second. I have not hesitated to repeat this wherever it seemed appropriate. I apologize if you find this annoying, but constant exposure to key points inevitably leads to better learning.

The third section deals with some common-sense ideas of time management applicable to all types of work, not only teaching. But as we all know, common sense is very rarely common practice. If you make these your common practice, you will work much more effectively and efficiently.

The book is laid out according to a well-defined principle. Each main sub-section has:

◆ an overview of the contents

◆ a paragraph or two discussing the context of the chapter

◆ the fine details

◆ a brief review of the main points

This book will help you control your time. You will find how to get more work done in less time with much less stress. You will have more time for yourself, your family, and your friends. No matter how happy you are now, you will be happier.

**Part One**

# The Time Management Mind-Set

**1**

# The 4 Secrets of Time

- ◆ Context
- ◆ The four secrets of time
- ◆ How the four secrets work
- ◆ A comparison
- ◆ A word of warning
- ◆ Review

## Context

This chapter outlines the essential knowledge base upon which you can build your time-management practices. Without this knowledge you will simply have a set of techniques which will work indifferently, if they work at all.

You must work hard to turn the words on the page

into a set of deeply held beliefs. Only then will you manage your time brilliantly.

## The 4 secrets of time

These four short little sentences are your key to successful time management. They take account of everything that you need in order to work effectively and efficiently.

1. Have an excellent reason.

2. Have an excellent plan.

3. Do the right thing.

4. Do the thing right.

They really are very simple. Just sixteen little words, but they convey great power.

If you miss out any of them, you will inevitably waste a great deal of your time. You need to think about this deeply and understand the full implications.

## How the 4 secrets work

### *Have an excellent reason*

According to Anthony Robbins (see Reading List) we always have one of two reasons for doing the things that we do. We either want to avoid pain or we want to generate pleasure.

The things that we do to avoid pain are the stressful things; we do them because we have to, and they don't give us a feeling of positive achievement. We often put these things off to the last minute and then do them in a rush with little care or thought. The quality is usually commensurate with the care that goes into them.

The things that we do to generate pleasure are those which make life worth living; they give us a feeling of exhilaration and real achievement. We do these things early and get them done with excellence because we have made an emotional investment and we want the benefit of the returns.

A life spent in avoiding pain and little else is not going to be very pleasurable. Everywhere is tedium and serving other people's needs at the expense of our own. The tasks are done to avoid criticism and trouble; simply to get out of uncomfortable situations and embarrassment.

A life spent in generating pleasure is a life well lived. There is the joy of achieving significance, of serving others and reaping the rewards of jobs well done. It is immensely satisfying to be able to reflect on a day's work and say with confidence that the day has been well spent.

Given the option, most people would choose the latter.

You DO have the option. It is your life and how you lead it is up to you and no one else. How you view the tasks that you have to do is your choice. If you view them as being pain avoidance, you will not enjoy them. If you view them as being pleasure generators, you will enjoy them.It is your mission statement that

'We always have one of two reasons for doing the things that we do. Avoid pain, generate pleasure' gives you the excellent reason for doing the job. If you have a definite mission to live out and a clear set of roles, values and principles, you have everything you need to see your way forwards. Your mission statement provides the compass which keeps you on course and gives you the confidence and clarity of vision to perform at the highest level.

A simple example is your classroom display. If you decorate your classroom simply to avoid pain from the boss or Ofsted, you will have no clear idea of what it is that you want to achieve and you will probably finish up with a colourful but sterile mishmash of posters and examples of students' work. You will spend many hours creating a mess and you won't be delighted with the results.

If, on the other hand, you have a vision of your classroom as being a place of joy and creative learning activity, you will have a clear vision of exactly what it is that you want to achieve. You will be able to create a wonderfully motivating and delightful environment in which the kids are stimulated and happy and which meets your educational aims and objectives.

Consider some of your other jobs: lesson planning, marking, report writing, etc. The mental attitude that you bring to the tasks that go to make up your job is completely under your control. Is the glass half empty or half full? Do you work to avoid pain or to generate pleasure?

## Have an excellent plan

If you are to spend your time well, you absolutely must have a clear and well-defined plan for how you use your time. You have to fit the tasks which need to be done into the time available for their completion. If you only plan the tasks and not the time, you will inevitably fail on both counts. You will fail to complete most of the tasks to a satisfactory standard and you will certainly fail to make the best use of your time.

Consider this: no one was ever consistently successful by accident. Success comes from consistently applying the right effort in the right way to an excellent plan.

## Plan your career

Map out your desired career progression. Put in the positions you want and the dates by which you want to reach these positions. Consider the experience you need, the extra qualifications you may need, the references you need and the personal qualities that are needed to go with the job.

## Plan your year, term, weeks, days and lessons

Have a very clear picture of what you want to achieve in the long, medium and short terms. You must have a clear vision of what you want your teaching to achieve for yourself and for the kids you teach. The long-term goals must be very clear and the medium and short-term goals must carry you onwards and forwards towards reaching those goals.

## Plan your ideal school, year group or department.

Spend some time deciding what your vision of your school really is. The school mission statement is your starting point for this. Decide on the changes that need to be made and the systems that need to be created to sustain the changes. Make a plan for achieving these goals. Put in dates and exact quality standards.

## Plan your classroom

Plan your classroom to be a stimulating and enjoyable learning and thinking environment for both yourself and the students. Have colourful posters both commercially produced and self-produced, the schemes of work (preferably in the form of concept maps or on time lines) so students can see their progress week by week, examples of students' work, concept maps of past, present and future work and maybe a photo gallery.

## Plan your life

You need a clear picture of what you want to achieve with your life. You are a multi-faceted individual. The only way that you can polish each of those facets and make them shine is if you take the time and make the effort to polish them for yourself. No one else is going to do it for you.

Your plan for all these things, and many others that you must work out for yourself, is the route map to guide you through your life.

The plan must include:

◆ the stages that need to be completed

◆ a quality definition (explicit or implicit)

◆ deadlines

# Every Minute Counts

A plan without a deadline is just a pipe dream. Your plan, remember, is all about getting things done ON TIME and IN TIME.

## *Do the right thing*

No one really cares about the quality of your vision, about your dreams and aspirations. No one cares about how carefully you have planned the work that you do. Ultimately, no one really cares about the class of your degree or the number of INSET sessions you have been on or the courses you have under your belt. These things are certainly of crucial importance, but they are only of importance to you.

The sole measure that anybody will ever apply to your work and your life is the results that you have achieved. And you only get results by action.

You get the results you want by applying tools to the raw materials. The raw materials are your thoughts and ideas. Your tools are the knowledge that you have and the skill with which you apply that knowledge. The raw materials are of little value by themselves. The tools are only of any use when they are used by a masterly hand.

It is actually the quality of the hand which is of the greater importance than the quality of the tool. David Bailey could take a better photograph using a 1935 Box Brownie camera than you or I could ever take using the most expensive and up-to-date camera in the world.

Tools expertly used by a highly skilled hand on first-class raw materials produce masterpieces.

The key is application. There are three simple rules:

- Apply your butt to the seat of the chair.
- Apply your concentration 100 per cent to the task.
- Apply your whole being to the task, start work and don't stop until you have completed it.

If you do this, you will naturally fall into the flow state. This is a delightful state characterized by relaxation and focus.

Results are the only things that count and the right results only ever flow from the right actions.

## *Do the thing right*

Jeffrey J. Mayer, one of the USA's leading time-management gurus, says, 'If you haven't got time to do it right first time, when are you going to find time to do it over again?'

You have to do the job right first time every time. The alternatives are that you either do it wrong and leave it wrong or you have to rework it. The first one produces substandard quality work, the second wastes time and effort. Neither is acceptable. You must have an eye for quality. Quality must be built into every single stage from design to production to delivery.

Quality means that the finished product is valued by the consumer and that it fulfils the need for which it was obtained. The finished product is, of course, the education that we make available to the students. If it is not a quality product, the consumer (student) will not want it or value it. That is a waste of your time.

Doing the thing right means getting the right degree of quality into everything that you do. Your plan must have an implicit or explicit quality standard built into it, and you must achieve exactly that standard. Neither too much nor too little. Too much is wasteful of resources, too little reduces the value.

## A comparison

I will compare you to a production entity, because that, in essence, is what you are. You produce education, and you are subject to exactly the same laws as a gigantic manufacturing industry or a single craftsman producing hand-made flower pots.

Any production entity needs:

- Leadership

- Management

- Production

- Quality control

**Leadership** is based on vision. By having an excellent reason for doing the things that you do, you create that vision. By having an excellent reason, you are providing yourself with self-leadership.

**Management** is based on having a clear plan and understanding of how to apply resources to production. By having a clear plan for yourself, you are providing yourself with self-management.

**Production** means getting the job done on time (meeting deadlines) and in time (using time intelligently hence reducing stress and costs and increasing productivity). Doing the right thing means taking care of production.

**Quality control** is checking that the production meets the expected quality BEFORE IT GOES OUT OF THE DOOR. Doing the thing right ensures that you have quality control systems in place.

These four secrets of time take care of all these things.

By adopting, adapting and applying these four secrets of time to yourself, you have re-created yourself as a one-person high-productivity entity!

You have quality, quantity, effectiveness and efficiency all built in to a single system.

## A word of warning

These secrets are presented as a nice linear little system. They are, of course, no such thing. There is a constant interplay of feedforward and feedback at every stage and even within stages. To pretend otherwise would be a damaging oversimplification. We are talking about a complex system (you!) and such systems need to be designed very carefully and maintained with even more care.

Here, more than anywhere else, there is an overriding need to use the *Adopt, Adapt, Apply* (3 As) approach. This is vital because you MUST buy in to these ideas. When you buy in to these ideas and design the system to suit yourself, you make it self-sustaining.

The leverage in this system is in the first secret; having an excellent reason. If you create your reason strongly enough and it is motivating enough, you will easily create the rest of the system to sustain itself.

## Review

- Remember that there are four essential secrets of using your time.

- If you miss out any one of these secrets, you will inevitably waste huge amounts of time.

- Have an excellent reason. This is the secret of self-leadership.

- Have an excellent plan. This is the secret of self-management.

- Do the right thing. This is the secret of productivity.

- Do the thing right. This is the secret of quality control.

## 2

# The 40-hour Week

- Context
- Commitment
- The deathbed scene
- The funeral scene
- Roles
- The designer week
- Review

## Context

Recent research by PricewaterhouseCoopers (PwC) has shown that the average working week for primary and secondary classroom teachers is about 52 hours. Their report also indicated that the average for equivalent-level professionals is about 44 hours. Similar research done by The Scottish Council for Research in Education (SCRE) gave similar results and reported that some teachers worked upwards of 60 hours per week.

Working weeks of 50 to 60 hours are quite unreasonable and ultimately unsustainable. A 35-hour week is probably not reachable.

I believe that a working week of 40 hours is reasonable – comparable to the workload of other professionals. It is also attainable as this chapter will show

This section deals with how to work a week of 40 high-productivity hours. This is quite some goal to achieve and won't be easy. If you are to achieve it, you must commit to it. Once you are absolutely committed to a goal, it becomes a simple matter to achieve it. No, I didn't say easy, I said simple. You are going to have to invest a great deal of effort and learn new ways of working.

## Commitment

It seems straightforward enough, doesn't it? If you spend less time at work, you get more time to spend with your family and friends. It looks like a very simple system.

The problem is that it doesn't work like that. Parkinson's Law (which was invented as a joke, but which turns out to be true) states that work expands to fill the time available for its completion.

What inevitably happens is that people who learn more efficient working practices get the work done faster. They then take on more work to fill up the freed-up time. They then find that they have no more time than before. They become depressed and go back to the old inefficient working practices. As they now have the same old practices plus more work (since it has become expected of them) they spend more time at work with more stress than ever before!

Our seemingly simple system with only two components (excessive work time and insufficient non-work time) actually has three components (add in Parkinson's Law). We need to add something to neutralize Parkinson's Law and so make it a simple two-component system again.

You've guessed it, you've got to add commitment. You have to commit to spending less time at work and more time for yourself, your family and friends. It's easy to say 'NO' to having an excessive workload when you have a stronger 'YES' to a fulfilling and happy home and social life.

You really don't need to trade off one against the other. You simply make a deeply felt and unshakeable commitment to reclaiming time from work and giving it to yourself, your family, your friends and your community.

Parkinson's Law is now completely neutralized. The same work will be easily compressed into less time. The time liberated is not available for extra work; it is committed to other uses.

Remember, you are not making a decision to shirk your responsibilities or to do the job in a slipshod or half-hearted way. Quite the opposite. You are committing to being a very highly effective and efficient teacher working 40 high-productivity hours a week and reaching the highest standard of excellence. You are also committing to using the time liberated from the job to benefit yourself, your family, your friends, your community etc.

You are committing to leading a full and happy life at work and away from work.

## The deathbed scene

Project yourself far into the future. Empathize and involve yourself with this very clearly. Invest your thoughts and emotions into this scene. Imagine yourself, many years from now, lying on your deathbed. Don't worry about it. You aren't in pain or even discomfort. You are simply coming to the end of a long life.

Surrounding you are your loved ones and closest friends. There they are, your spouse and children, maybe a few grandchildren and others from your extended family. Also there are some of your fellow retirees and people from your community. You are able to talk with them lucidly.

Consider the things that have filled your life. The things you have done either alone or in the company of your family and other loved ones.

Consider the things you may say to those presently with you.

Take two clean pages in your notebook and make lists.

One page is: I wish I hadn't spent so much time _____ing _____.

E.g. I wish I hadn't spent so much time attending pointless meetings.

The other page is: I wish I'd spent more time _____ing _____.

E.g. I wish I'd spent more time talking with my kids.

The first list gives a clear indication of those things that you need to spend less time doing. The second tells you where to spend more time NOW, while you are still here to do it. Since you must die sometime, you want to die happy. What adjustments do you need to make to your life so that you can leave without regret when the time comes?

Most people find that they need to spend very much less time at work and very much more with their family and friends. This little exercise helps you focus on the important, people-centred things and rather less on the urgent ones.

## The funeral scene

Too many of us go through life without any clear idea of what it is that we want to achieve.

This is another exercise which will help you focus on the important things in life and show you things that may have escaped getting the full attention that they deserve. The problem with importance is that it is often buried deeply under the urgent and pressing things of life.

Imagine your funeral. Many people have gathered together to join in celebration of your life and your achievements. There is sadness, of course, and even tears. But there is more than that; for those people there who have had the pleasure of sharing parts of your life with you, there is gratitude in abundance.

There are four people delivering the eulogy.

One from your family. This person will speak about what it was like to be a member of your extended

17

family. There will be reminders of joyful occasions and some more poignant ones only of significance to family. Some of the things said will raise a laugh as people recognize the idiosyncrasies that made up such a large part of your life.

One from your friends. This person will speak about you as a friend; a person who could be called upon in times of dire need, but one who was fun to be with; one who gave friendship and was not afraid to call for support in times of need.

One from your cohort of retirees. This person will speak about what it was like to work with you. This person will tell about the advice and help you gave and the way you acted as a team member, a leader, a mentor, a creative problem-solver and a steady rock in times of trouble.

One from your community. This person will speak about your contributions to society, about the work you did both publicly and behind the scenes to help those less well-off and fortunate than you. He will speak of the lasting legacy that you helped to create and how so many people, not closely connected with you, will be saddened to hear of your passing.

What exactly do you want these four speakers to say? How do you want to be remembered?

Take your notebook and write a short eulogy that you would like each of these people to deliver. What do you want all these people and the many others who know you to remember about you?

You need to be very focused on the important things in life – the people-centred things.

You now have a very clear guide for the way that you want to live your life and the things that you want to do with it. What do you want to be left by your graveside? Flowers or a copy of the your school's Ofsted report?

## Roles

To deepen the desire to work a 40-hour week, let's look at the roles you play in life outside work. You must pay due attention to them or they will just slip away from you. Remember the funeral? You have these roles. You must commit to them.

All the world's a stage, wrote William Shakespeare. Ah, yes, and we all play many different roles which change from moment to moment. In the space of a few minutes with my kids this afternoon I've been a peacemaker, a nurse, a playmate, a learning mentor, a football coach and a detective on a missing dolly investigation. ('When did you last see her? ... What were you doing? ... Where were you?' etc. The case was eventually solved!) They are all important roles in the overall role of being a daddy.

(I wonder if my daughter will remember the case when she prepares her eulogy for me. Maybe not, but it will still be there, deep in her other-than-conscious mind as a happy memory of a loving dad.)

Take a clean sheet of paper in your notebook and write in the middle of it 'ROLES'. Make a concept shower of all the roles you play in every area of your life.

What are your five or six most important overall roles in life? Try to consider broad categories rather than narrow ones. You may, for example be a golfer, a

19

footballer, a cyclist and go for a run twice a week. Group them together under a single heading of 'Sports player'. In the same way, don't consider parent, sibling, child etc. as separate roles, but group them as 'Family member'.

Now, on another clean sheet, prepare yourself a pie chart like the one shown here.

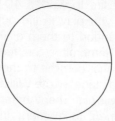

Decide on your major roles in life and determine the proportion of your non-working life that you want each one to fill. Naturally, each one takes time and the question is always going to be how you find the time. That's the next section.

## The designer week

Your aim is to get your job done in 40 hours Monday to Friday and have completely free weekends. Other people can do it, and so can you. Yes, your job is important and should be done assiduously and to the very best of your ability. But so are your family and friends important. They deserve to have at least an equally large part of your commitment.

A vital idea to get hold of is that having a reasonable working week is not stealing time from the job to give to your family. Sadly, that is the idea that all too many of us carry around in our heads. It is precisely the opposite. You are entitled to your family and they are entitled to you. It is an unreasonable and ultimately unsustainable workload which is stealing time from you and you family.

In the five days Monday to Friday there are 24 × 5 hours = 120 hours. Of those hours you should aim to spend 40 hours in sleep and deep relaxation, 40 hours at work and 40 hours for yourself, family and friends. The weekends are completely your own.

Of the 40 hours for yourself, family and friends, much of that time is spent on the mundane matters of living. It takes time to get to work, to prepare meals, to wash clothes, go shopping, clean the house, ferry the kids to swimming, etc. This probably amounts to about 15 hours all together.

Let's have a look at the 80 waking hours of an average 5-day working week.

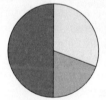  

If you spend 40 hours on the job, you have 40 hours, take away the 15 mundane hours for everything else. That leaves 25 hours.

If you spend 50 hours on the job, you have 30 hours, take away the 15 mundane hours for everything else. That leaves 15 hours.

If you spend 60 hours on your job, you have 20 hours, take away the 15 mundane hours for everything else. That leaves about 5 hours.

You can see quite clearly from the diagrams; time saved on the job is repaid many times over in the proportion of your time liberated for yourself, your family and friends. Reducing your working week by 33 per cent increases your free time by a massive 500 per cent

## Assigning time to non-work

You have now committed to spending 25 hours a week for yourself, family and friends. How are you going to use that time?

You already have a pie chart showing the relative importance of the roles that you play in life. It is now a fairly simple matter to assign the amount of time that each of those roles deserves.

You may have decided that 40 per cent of your time is family time, for example. OK. 40 per cent of 25 hours is 10 hours. You have to organize your non-work time to spend 10 hours a week in family activity. That's about 2 hours a night. That's 2 hours a night in quality time spent connecting with your family and doing the things that make family life so very rewarding.

You may well have decided that 10 per cent of your time is down to self-maintenance. 10 per cent of 25 hours is $2\frac{1}{2}$ hours. You now have to commit to spending that time every week on activities that are going to support you and maintain good health. It may be that you decide on 30 minutes per night or $1\frac{1}{4}$ hours twice a week or whatever. The exact details are up to you and your preferences. The only important thing is that you do it and you stick to it.

Take a clean page in your notebook and design your evenings around your regular activities and make sure that you get all your different roles in place and sufficient time dedicated to each one.

## Making the mundane into fun

If you add to that a strong desire to make the mundane into fun, much more time can be liberated.

Make time spent shopping into fun time. Give yourself a very strict time and money limit as to how much of both you will spend. After the shopping is over, take the family to Macdonald's or buy the stuff for a picnic and go and sit in the park for thirty minutes.

Try making mealtimes into real quality time. Get help preparing the meal and laying the table; get everyone to do their bit. Turn off the TV and have a candle-lit dinner.

Don't allow breakfast TV, but talk about what you hope to achieve with the new day that you have been given. Spend twenty minutes real quality time talking about what you did when you get home and listening to what everybody else has done.

Design your days so that the mundane becomes shared mundane and therefore much more fun.

It is absolutely vital that you plan activities to go into your newly liberated time. If you don't, it will inevitably happen that you find work to fill it up. If this happens, you will have wasted the whole exercise. The time liberated must remain liberated. Moreover, it must be liberated for YOUR benefit.

## *Assigning time to the working week*

You are committed to a 40-hour working week. You need to assign time to the different tasks that you do to ensure that you are able to achieve this and maintain it.

We've already seen Parkinson's Law: Work expands to fill the time available for its completion.

I'm now proposing Papworth's Law: Work can always be compressed to fit into the time available for its completion provided that (i) the determination to achieve this aim is strong enough and (ii) the requisite knowledge and skills are available.

This section is about the determination. The rest of the book is about the requisite knowledge and skills.

It's time to make another pie chart.

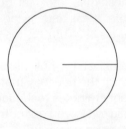

The chart represents the 40 hours that you are going to spend at work. A little over half of this is probably going to be classroom time. You now need to assign time to the other tasks that you need to do in order to fulfil your roles as a teacher.

Make up the pie chart for yourself using your roles and your ideas about how you should apportion your time. Then make up a table and put in the number of hours on each task.

| Role | Time (hours) |
|------|--------------|
|      |              |
|      |              |
|      |              |
|      |              |

The problem now is to ensure that:

◆ your time is well apportioned

◆ you can complete the tasks in the time allowed

Both of these require a degree of deep thought and dedication on your part. You will apply the 3 As to this and make sure that it suits you, your school, your classes, etc.

## Life time = work time + non-work time

You now have an excellent blueprint for the way that you are going to spend your time. Naturally, you're not going to be a slave to the system and you won't be able to spend every single week in this way. That's not the point.

The point is that you have invested heavily of yourself into considering very carefully just how you are going to use the time of your life to achieve the things that you need and want to achieve. The stage is set for a revolutionary way of reaching excellence AND reaching it in a sensible and sustainable working and non-working week.

The result can only be achievement and a better balanced life.

This just happens to be my personal definition of happiness. You have your own personal definition of happiness, but I think that you will probably agree that mine is not too far off the mark.

## Review

- You need to be committed before you can succeed.

- Consider how you want to be remembered, and then live your life that way.

- Your working week consists of 120 hours:
  40 for work
  40 for rest and sleep
  40 for yourself, your family and friends.

- Design yourself an ideal working week, and then do it.

- The key to living a happy and fulfilling life is to identify your most important roles and live them to the full.

I always phone home before leaving work giving my ETA so the family is ready when I walk in through the door. (Daddy coming home has got to be a big deal.) When I get back from work, I stop the engine, turn off the radio and sit in the car for about two or three minutes and relax. I make a conscious effort to allow all the stresses and strains of the day to just melt away. I focus on what I'm going to say about my day to my wife and kids. I make sure that these are always positive things, no one wants to hear grumbling.

When I get in I greet my wife and kids and spend 15 minutes in just plain family time. We all share our experiences and find out how we've been getting on. I ask the kids what they've learned in school and about their friends and their music lessons, sports and the other things that are important to them. I reconnect with my wife and she tells me about her day. I try to find something funny about my day and share it with them all. Meanwhile we are all fussing with the dog who wants to be a part of it all.

The family bonding is a little bit stronger.

What a wonderful start to the evening!

There's no way that I'm ever going to bring work home with me. I'm committed to spending my home-time at home doing home things and cementing home relationships.

To paraphrase Kipling: home is home and work is work and ne'er the twain shall meet.

**Part Two**

# Essential Skills

3

# Weekly Planning

- ◆ Context
- ◆ What it is
- ◆ Why you need it
- ◆ How to do it
- ◆ The lists
- ◆ Review

## Context

The way you plan your weeks is going to determine how you spend your weeks. If you plan for high effectiveness and efficiency, you'll get it. If you plan in a random way or even fail to plan at all but just 'go with the flow' you will inevitably waste huge amounts of your time doing unfocused busy-ness.

Between 10 and 30 minutes spent in planning your week in outline will save you many hours.

## What it is

Weekly planning takes care of both the medium-term (weekly) and the short-term (daily) planning, both at the same time. You do this by planning out your week in advance putting in blocks of time for 'chunks' of work. You leave a little slack in the system to allow for the daily eventualities and for emergency re-assigning of blocks, if needs be.

## Why you need it

It is generally held that time spent in planning is repaid a minimum of four times and up to as much as ten times over. Thus ten minutes spent planning can save you between 40 and 100 minutes of unproductive 'busy-ness' time. For a teacher, it is likely to be nearer 10 times because of the nature of the job.

Most other groups of professionals have a limited number of roles to play at work. Each role is well-defined and it is fairly simple to assign the necessary time to each one. This is most certainly not the case in teaching, and this is where our major problems of time management lie. Quite apart from teaching and PPMR, we are policemen and women, social workers, paper pushers, nurses, artists and writers, decorators, etc. The problems are directly caused by the disjointed nature of the tasks.

When you can sit down and work steadily at an extended task, you can accomplish a huge amount of work in a very short time. But as we know this is not so in teaching. We have to be aware of the issue and do our best to address it.

It is excellent and intelligent planning that does so!

## How to do it

You will spend somewhere between ten and thirty minutes each and every week making yourself an outline plan of what the week will look like. Naturally, you will take into account things like staff meetings, parents' evenings, clubs and the like which are fixed.

The next stage is to see what other large and important tasks need to be completed and get them in place. You will now have a good idea of what the week holds in store and be able to plan in the other things that need to be done. Think of it like laying crazy paving. You have to get the big pieces in first and then fit in the smaller ones around them. The idea is identical when organizing your time.

The numerous tasks themselves are disjointed, but the general nature of them is not. The skill of planning tasks of this nature is to 'chunk' them so that as many tasks which require the same approach, equipment, etc. are done at the same time.

If you have a pile of paperwork to do, for instance, you will plan to get it done at one sitting. You will then deliver the papers or file them or whatever at one time. If you complete a piece of paperwork and then stop to file it, return to complete another one then dash off to deliver it, return to complete a third and then write the envelope and take it to the office for posting, etc. ... Well, you can see the problem. The tasks are about as disjointed as they can be.

When you 'chunk' your tasks, you give yourself the opportunity to get into a flow state which immediately increases your efficiency by upwards of 50 per cent.

In the paperwork example above, you first of all prepare your working space to make sure you have all the tools of the trade handy. You will lay out all the papers and decide on the order to tackle them. You will then tackle them quickly and efficiently. Once they are completed, you will action them as required.

Similarly, if you need face-to-face contact with individuals, plan to see them in quick succession in a single swoop. Take your logbook with you and make a quick note of the date, nature and outcomes of each conversation. Again, you can then go back to your desk and action the outcomes as required.

In an ideal world, you would have a single planning tool and a single logging tool.

You may have noticed that it's not an ideal world. Your job, then, is to make your little corner of it as ideal as you can.

## The lists

### *The Master List*

This list contains every single thing that you need to do that week and the coming weeks. There is no attempt to order the items at all. They are simply there to remind you that they need to be done at some time. Every time a new task appears, it goes on the list. The list is an organic thing. It grows as you add tasks and diminishes as you complete them and strike them off. It's a good idea to make a note of the deadline if one exists alongside the task.

This is where you 'store' the tasks that need to be done. You will call them off into the 'to do' list (next section) as and when they need to be done and you have engineered the free time to do them.

There are few things more rewarding than crossing an item off a list. Do it with a bold flourish using a coloured pen and feel the glow of satisfaction. I know of one person who sometimes gets jobs to be done immediately without the chance to write them on the list. After the task is completed, he writes it on the list and immediately crosses it off just for the buzz of doing it and as a record that it has been done.

If there are any tasks remaining uncompleted at the end of the week, they are transferred to the list for the following week.

Using this list, you have automatically ensured that nothing slips through the cracks, nothing gets lost, nothing needs to be left to the last minute and nothing gets forgotten. You relieve your memory and de-stress, as you know that everything you need to do is written in a single place.

## *The prioritized To Do list*

You will create this list either first thing every morning or last thing in the evening of the previous day. (It's a personal choice. The only VITAL thing is that you do it.) You inspect the Master List and decide which of the tasks can be done that day. Naturally, you'll do your very best to 'chunk' them as suggested above to ensure efficiency.

At this stage, you MUST prioritize the tasks. This may seem a simple and straightforward process, but there are pitfalls for the unwary. There are a number of ways of prioritizing, some of which assign a numerical value to urgency, importance, relevance to roles, etc. These methods are probably more important to CEOs and merchant bankers than to humble teachers like ourselves. I only mention it to highlight that prioritizing IS important and has been the topic of intense study.

Each task should be assigned a code:

AA = MEGA-URGENT – MUST BE DONE TODAY TO AVOID CATASTROPHE!!!! (There should be very few of these. They can be almost completely eliminated by good planning all round.)

A = Urgent – Today is the best time. Leaving this until tomorrow could lead to great inconvenience. You can't be certain that disaster won't strike tomorrow and leave you without the time to do it. (You don't want a reputation for tardiness.)

B = Important – The sooner the better. This is something that relates to your roles and goals. If you don't get it done soon it could become an A or an AA or it will prevent you from reaching the standard of excellence that you're aiming for.

C = Better today – as it's then out of the way, but it can be put off without great inconvenience.

Q = A Quickie – Something that can be fitted in at a convenient time. It's always a good idea to set aside a decent period of time to get these done all at once. Remember each one crossed off the master list gives a real sense of achievement.

Urgent, in this sense, means that there is a strong time pressure associated with the task. Getting reports out on time is the obvious example, but there are thousands more. Whenever another person is involved in the chain, urgency is usually a factor.

Important, in this sense, means something that relates directly to your roles and goals. A good example of this is keeping your classroom display up-to-date and looking fresh and occasional tidying the stockroom. The other obvious one is planning!

As long as you pay enough attention to the Bs, Cs and the Qs, the number of As and AAs is going to diminish as they are dealt with before they become urgent. You can probably see how this system works as a wonderful stress reliever. The stressful jobs are those that fall into the A and AA categories. As you have a system for dealing with them, they become fewer and fewer and hence much less stressful.

Depending on the time you have available, you may want to do some of the As and Bs at the same time if they fall into the same broad category (e.g. paperwork). As with everything, you need to use a good degree of intelligence and use the system creatively.

Please note that the AAs can never be completely

eliminated as they are very frequently caused by other people's bad time management. Where they are caused by your own poor management, learn the lesson and get things done in plenty of time.

Naturally, part of your planning will be to create a time for planning. Planning in the long term, medium term and short term. In an ideal world, long and medium-term planning is a collaborative thing done with colleagues. An increasing number of schools are creating time slots for this to be done. Individual short-term planning, of course, is usually done individually, but can easily be a collaborative thing where parallel classes are taught by different teachers.

## *Roles list*

Because you are a teacher and have so many different jobs to do it is all too easy to lose sight of the reason for doing them. We do a lot of things simply because we have always done them. Similarly, we have done things in a certain way simply because that's the way we do them. We all evolve along certain lines.

Each week, make a list of the roles on which you are going to make a special effort to concentrate. If you are a form tutor, for example, you may decide to make a very special effort to connect with some of the more diffident kids one week. Don't worry about the kids suffering withdrawal symptoms the next week, they will naturally help you continue.

Similarly, write yourself a list of goals that you want to achieve each week. If you teach a science subject, for example, you might really concentrate on the personal aspects of science. Perhaps you might spend a little time on the biography of Michael Faraday or the relevance of cell division to disease, etc.

You may want to focus on one or two particular roles every single week. Maybe they are something so central to your mission that you never want to lose sight of them. You are using your plan to give life to your reason for doing things. You are not allowing yourself to lose sight of the importance of your job and the knowledge, skills, qualities, principles and added value that you can bring to it.

# Review

- Planning time is repaid between 4 and 10 times over.

- It is likely to be nearer to 10 times for a teacher because of the disjointed nature of the tasks.

- Have a single planning tool that covers classroom teaching and all the other associated tasks.

- Use a Master List to record all tasks as they become known. The tasks are not ordered.

- Use a daily To Do list. Prioritize the tasks AA, A, B, C, Q.

- Differentiate between Urgent and Important.

- Keep track of your roles and ensure that importance is considered, not just urgency.

**4**

# 5-minute Lesson Planning

- Context
- Five-minute lesson planning
- Why you need it
- How it works
- Stage 1 – Thinking about your lesson plan
- Stage 2 – Making your lesson plan
- Summary of the 5-minute lesson planning technique
- Review

## Context

The aim of this section to show you how to plan an excellent brain-based lesson in five minutes or less. Your lesson plan is there to help your lessons fulfil their major purpose; to help the students learn effectively and efficiently. A well-planned lesson cannot be other than far superior to a poorly planned one.

The output of this technique is perfectly congruent and aligned with the recommendations of DfES.

A key question to ask yourself is: 'Who should be doing most of the work in my lessons? Me or the children?' If you answered, 'Me,' you're wrong! Design and plan your lessons so that the kids are doing MUCH more work than you are. Kids learn best when they are fully and deeply involved with the lesson. That idea should inform your planning as much as anything else.

## 5-minute lesson planning

Quite apart from the requirements of Ofsted, the boss, your HoD and even your own requirements, your lesson plans are primarily for your students' benefit. The ideal lesson must be planned, not with teaching in mind, but with learning being the first and foremost consideration.

Your lesson plan determines to a very great extent how you will teach a lesson. Nature determines how the students learn it. There must be a very high degree of congruence between your teaching and the students' learning if your lessons are going to be effective and efficient. Your lesson plan must therefore go with the natural abilities of learners.

Remember that your lesson plan has to cater for the top-down learners and the bottom-up learners. Lesson planning is planning to create an environment in which learning (NOT just teaching) can take place. This technique always produces lessons which do exactly that.

## Why you need it

You need lesson planning skills in order to plan excellent lessons, of course. But there is more to it than that. You don't want to be spending your entire life doing it. This technique prepares the lessons you want, and does it in five minutes or less.

## How it works

Remember: everything is created twice. First comes the mental creation, then follows the physical creation.

This system works because you do your thinking first and then follow that with the pencil and paper writing.

You need to do this in order to work effectively and efficiently.

(i) You do your thinking according to a very simple and powerful system. This clarifies exactly what you want the lesson to achieve and look like according to educationally sound principles.

(ii) You then follow this by placing your excellent thinking into an educationally sound lesson shape.

You have separated your work into two distinct areas and you have a sound and simple system for each one.

## Stage 1 – Thinking about your lesson plan

This is, of course, crucial to the whole lesson. You must choose and define your overall aim as carefully as possible. Any fudging or lack of clarity here is going to be fatal to the clarity of the lesson. More often than not, of course, it can be lifted or adapted straight from the national curriculum.

## *Think 1*

Once you have your aim very clearly established you need to think about three things.

- Warmer – to get the students warmed up and to create a good start to the lesson.

- Objectives – to make it very clear exactly what is going to be addressed in the lesson.

- Learning outcomes – so you know exactly what the students will learn in terms of knowledge, understanding and skills.

   Let's look at these one by one.

### Warmer

The warmer is essentially a short (5 to 10-minute) high-involvement activity designed to get the students' mental muscles pumped up and ready for action.

   It will usually involve a whole-class approach and will be an essentially mental exercise as opposed to mainly writing or reading. Students may be involved in a solitary thinking activity or possibly a group activity with a well-defined outcome.

   The warmer may be specifically linked to the rest of the lesson either directly (in that it leads in to the remainder of the lesson) or indirectly (in that it re-activates knowledge or skills that will be required at some point in the lesson). This is by no means essential. It could be simply a quick revision of last week's work or just a little puzzle to get the brain juices flowing. Another use is to reinforce the things that need to be repeated 'little and often'.

No matter what they are or are not, they MUST be slick and well-controlled. Warmers must not be allowed to drag on or get the students bogged down in things which are not productive. They need to be just as carefully planned, executed and directed as any other part of the lesson.

These warmers are a particularly fruitful area for co-operation between teachers of parallel classes. You should create a file of suitable activities and try to persuade colleagues to buy in to equal investment and ownership.

## Objectives

Planning with objectives foremost in mind moves the focus to learning first and to teaching second. This is just as it should be. The only important question is what the students learn. Learning is the treasure. Teaching gives the key that unlocks the treasure chest!

Think very carefully about how you can make three very clear and meaningful objectives. As long as your aim is clear, you can get away with a bit of honest fudging here. If you find that you really have five objectives, slim them down by combining some of them. If you only have two, split one of them into two parts.

41

There does seem to be quite a lot of confusion about the precise meaning of an objective. To put it as simply as possible, an objective is a hook (of knowledge, understanding, attitude or skill) that students can use to hang the rest of their learning from.

The reason that you need exactly three objectives is because everybody able to attend school has the capacity to remember three things (as long as they are paying attention and are involved in the lesson!). Memory works best by associating knowledge. If the three objectives are well remembered, then other information will also be remembered by association.

When I say that there should be three objectives in a lesson, there is no suggestion that students should learn only three things. Indeed, in a French lesson, for example, you might reasonably expect some students to learn twenty or more new vocabulary items.

Objectives are frequently written on the following stems:

- know/realize that ... (for knowledge, facts, formulae, equations, etc.)

- understand how/why ... (understanding concepts, reasons, etc.)

- be able to ... (for skills in using: knowledge, techniques, manipulations, analyses, etc.)

- be aware of ... (for attitudes, principles and values, etc.)

Using these stems helps avoid the pitfall of writing activities instead of objectives. They are attention-focusing devices.

When you write your objectives, keep in mind simple and precise questions that each and every student can answer during and at the end of the lesson.

There is no question that the less able will be able to answer only the first, the middle ability answer the first two and the stars of the group answering all three. Students of all abilities will be able to answer all three. The differences between students of differing abilities will lie in the amount of learning that each student will be able to hang from each of these three hooks. These are described as ...

## Learning outcomes

Learning outcomes are always defined in terms of what all students, most students and some students will have learned by the end of the lesson. It is vital to think in these terms to ensure that every single student will have gained a significant amount of learning from giving you their time and effort in attending and participating fully in your lesson.

You will define the learning outcomes for each of the objectives.

There is a lot of confusion between objectives and learning outcomes, but there really is a very big difference between them. They are NOT parallel concepts. In fact they are orthogonal. ALL students will be expected to achieve ALL the objectives. The differences will lie in the amount of learning (= differentiated learning outcomes) that each student will be able to attach to each of the objectives.

|  | Objective 1 | Objective 2 | Objective 3 |
|---|---|---|---|
| All students |  |  |  |
| Most students |  |  |  |
| Some students |  |  |  |

You now have a very deep understanding of exactly what it is that the students will learn. The next step is to think about what you are going to do to help them learn it!

## Think 2

You have invested a great deal of thought into the learning part of the equation. Now is time to do the thinking that you need about the teaching part of the job. Consider the range of Presentation techniques, Practice activities and Resources available to you. (I call these PPR.)

Consider the three major learning styles: visual, auditory and kinaesthetic (VAK). You need to include elements in the lesson which are going to appeal to all these three learning styles.

Remember the formula for learning:

- See it
- Hear it

* Say it
* Do it

Students must get the opportunity to use their own personal amalgam of VAK learning styles and:

* read and see pictures, diagrams, realia, etc.
* hear you and others talk about the details
* express their own ideas, opinions and feelings
* manipulate things and/or ideas to create something of significance using their new learning or revision

## Presentation techniques

Prepare a large range of presentation techniques that you know so well that you can adapt any one of them to any materials. Some will, of course, be more suited to some things than others.

Make a concept shower of all the different presentation techniques you know. You'll probably find that you actually know of ten or more, but only regularly use about four of them. You may find it helpful to make this concept shower with one or two colleagues.

## Practice activities

Prepare a very large range of practice activities that you know so well that you can adapt them to anything. The same argument as in the previous paragraph applies here as well. Make a concept shower.

Once you have these concept showers, stick them up on the wall above your desk or keep them in your lesson plans file. You need to be able to consult these quickly to make sure that you keep using the full variety of techniques you know and don't get stuck in a rut using just the ones that are your favourites.

## Resources

Prepare yourself by knowing the textbook inside out and back to front. (And upside down and inside out, if you like.) Be just as aware of all the supplementary materials that your department and the library has to offer.

You need to spend time getting to know what exists already. If you don't, you'll inevitably waste huge amounts of time and effort in seeking out materials when you should be focused on other things.

I cannot stress this too strongly: know the materials that you can call on at any time. Your department should have a list of them. If they haven't, start one for yourself and persuade the other members of your team to buy in to the task. I'm not pretending for one moment that this is going to be an easy task. It will take a huge amount of time and commitment. The point is that it is time which is relatively low-stress and the payback is incalculable in added value to you and as a time saver.

This file will be organic and grow with you as you get to spend more time on importance and less on urgency. It will be your primary resource for ideas and for increasing your creativity as you learn to adapt materials more easily. You will also learn how to exploit materials more effectively, but that's another book.

If you know the materials that you have available, you need NEVER EVER waste your time re-inventing the wheel. Thousands of teachers and textbook writers have already done it for you. It is there for the asking. Your school has spent a fortune on these resources. Use them.

Let me stress that this preparation of PPR is crucial to the five-minute aspect of the system. Once you have this in place, you can simply plug your thinking straight into the lesson plan format, as will be explained shortly.

## Stage 2 – Making your lesson plan

Lessons must have a clear shape. This makes life much easier for you AND for the students. There are three clearly identifiable stages.

1. Warmer (5 to 10 min)

2. Main teaching activity (30 to 45 min)

3. Plenary session (10 min)

Plus homework is an important consideration.

The times given are typical rather than highly prescriptive.

## 1 Warmer

This has been covered in some detail above. Don't forget the essential features; it must be short, sharp and engaging.

You will allow between five and ten minutes for this part of the lesson.

## 2 Main teaching activity

This part of the lesson, which is between 30 and 45 minutes will be split into three parts:

- Overview
- Preview
- Inview

### Overview

This is a very quick look at the title and the aim of the lesson and why and how it fits into the grand scheme of things. Because you have given the kids the entire syllabus outline previously, you can make reference to how far along you are and any relationships backwards and forwards. This should take no more than two minutes, but they are two incredibly important minutes.

### Preview

The objectives of the lesson are explained and clear questions are set. If the questions are kept in mind, the answers will be looked for without any more input from you. The objectives are written on the board so they are in THE UPPER LEFT-HAND VISUAL FIELD of the students whenever they look at the board. This is VITAL. This should be not more than two or three minutes

(Whenever you are trying to remember something, your eyes move around almost as if looking inside the brain. If you are looking to remember something you have seen, can you guess where your eyes move? That's right: your eyes move to the upper left visual field. If it is written there in the first place, it is MUCH easier to find later.)

## Inview(s)

The inview is the place where the meat of the lesson is located. Here is the learning of new things (knowledge, understanding, skills or attitudes) or revision.

Depending upon the nature of the topic and the objectives you may:

- have a single inview addressing all three objectives at once

- have two inviews addressing two objectives at once and the third by itself, or

- have three inviews if you deal with each objective in turn

Each of the inviews addresses the objectives using the following order:

- re-define objective(s) (refer to the board)

- presentation

- concept check (followed by re-presentation if needed)

- controlled practice followed by freer practice and free practice

- feedback

- remedial input if needed and feedback/review

Of course, you will keep on using feedforward and feedback to other elements of the subject and other subjects at irregular times. This is needed to add interest and to make sure that the students never lose sight of the big picture and the other elements that go up to make the big picture.

## 3 Plenary session (review)

This is where you wrap up the lesson and review as much as possible of what has happened in the lesson. It should be about ten minutes or so of high-involvement time.

The three objectives are checked again for complete understanding. You can do this by re-asking your objective questions. Don't think for a moment that you only need to ask one question one time to one student.

You may also wish to make a REARVIEW and an ONVIEW to see how the lesson relates to what has been learned in the past and what is going to come in the future. This helps to keep things in perspective and to solidify the feeling of progress being made.

Another very valuable part of a plenary session is to ask students to reflect upon their learning. Ask what they found enjoyable or boring, easy or difficult, relevant or irrelevant. Ask what strategies they used to learn and what strategies they might use in the future to improve their learning.

You may do these things as a whole-class activity or students may confer in groups and then report back to you and the class.

## Homework

The homework set must, of course, be relevant to the lesson and be doable. (There are few things more de-motivating than impossible homework tasks.)

### Summary of Stage 2

If you look at this system, it is clear how it works.

First of all, you are warming up the students' mental muscles. This motivates them and prepares them for learning.

The next stage is that the information is presented in a way that appeals to both top-down learners and bottom-up learners. It is sketching out the lesson and then progressively filling in detail until the final clear picture emerges for the top-downers and follows a logical and well-understood progression for the bottom-uppers. It is, as I said before, perfectly congruent with the way that learning occurs.

Finally, the learning is reinforced by checking that the lesson hangs together as an integrated whole.

The primacy effect is used to great advantage with the warmer and setting of objectives. The recency effect is utilized by the plenary session and the Von Restorff effect is used by returning to objectives, making excellent presentations and having stimulating practice activities.

The whole of the teaching time is well-used and learning takes place.

## Summary of the 5-minute lesson planning technique

You will find that this technique is incredibly fast and flexible. As long as you have a good variety of presentation techniques and practice techniques, no two lessons need ever be the same. As long as you know the materials available, you can use a large variety of them in different lessons.

| Aim + 3 Objectives | | |
|---|---|---|
| Presentation techniques + Practice activities + Resources | | |
| Warmer | Body of lesson | Plenary |
| Homework | | |

The overall shape of each and every lesson is identical, but as far as the students are concerned, there is a huge variety of different activities and learning methods.

The context of the lesson in the overall scheme of things is made clear. They are prepared for a learning experience, they learn it, and their learning is checked at the end of each lesson.

The test I always apply to this at the end of a lesson is: 'Tarquin, what will you say to your mum/dad/caregiver when they ask you what you learned in school today?' If Tarquin gives me back the three objectives I'd set at the start of the lesson and shows that he's related to them, I reckon he's learned it. And that is, when all is said and done, the point of the whole exercise.

Because the teaching process is congruent with the learning process, they complement each other. Both teaching and learning are far more effective and efficient. And that is what time management is all about.

## Review

- Think about learning first and foremost.

- Do your thinking first.

- Think about: your aims, 3 objectives, learning outcomes and the warmer.

- Remember PPR: Presentations techniques, Practice activities and Resources.

- Have a range of different presentation techniques ready to use.

- Have a range of practice activities ready to use.

- Have an intimate knowledge of the resource materials available for you to use.

## Every Minute Counts

- Make posters of PPR and put them on the wall above your desk.

- NEVER re-invent the wheel.

- Do your writing second.

- Slot your thinking into an excellent educationally sound lesson format.

- Aim to plan lessons in ten minutes and then, when you understand the system, cut it down progressively to five minutes.

# 5

# Marking

- Context
- Why you do it
- Different approaches
- Speeder uppers
- Review

## Context

According to studies conducted by Pricewaterhouse-Coopers, the NUT and SCRE, the average weekly time spent on marking is between 4 and 6 hours. That represents between 20 and 30 per cent of the non-teaching working week. That's about an hour a day. As long as the value of the exercise is sufficiently high, the figure is reasonable.

My own research shows that for certain groups of teachers and individual teachers, the load is considerably in excess of this. I know of individuals for whom the figure is 12 to 15 hours weekly. This is a completely unreasonable figure no matter what the value. Marking must be effective and efficient. Effective in this case means that it does the job that it is intended to do. Efficient, of course, means that it gets done in the minimum time commensurate with superb quality.

The output of the techniques suggested here is perfectly aligned with 'The Black Box' approach of Professor Paul Black *et al*.

# Why you do it

Marking certainly has value for you as a teacher in that it gives you valuable feedback. It has value for the parent in that it is evidence that Tarquin's work is being regularly monitored. It is valuable for the school in that it gives the same evidence.

But where is the value to Tarquin? Can you think of any greater waste of time than you spending 300 S (= 5 minutes) marking Tarquin's book only to have the dear boy spending 300 mS inspecting the mark, grunting approval or disappointment (or even worse, indifference) and then never looking at it again?

Where is the educational value in that? The return on your investment is zero. That is very poor time management.

If you are going to spend your time in giving Tarquin feedback, he should spend AT LEAST the same amount of time learning from it. If he doesn't, I suggest that the greatest part of the value of marking is wasted.

# Different approaches

We need to create a marking system which fulfils the following criteria:

- It gives you, the teacher, accurate feedback on a large number of issues.

- It reassures the parents/caregivers that work is being accurately and consistently monitored and sufficient individual attention is being given.

- It reassures the school management that work is being accurately and consistently monitored and sufficient individual attention is being given.

- It helps the pupil understand strengths and weaknesses, to build on the former and eliminate the latter.

- It is done efficiently (i.e. quickly) in order to get a good return on your investment of time.

There are several methods of marking:

## Complete marking

Every single page is examined in ultra-fine detail. Each significant point (positive or negative) is highlighted in some way. The highlight should indicate something meaningful and helpful, not just be a mark on a page. Each page may be initialled to indicate that it has been inspected. At least one helpful and pertinent comment is written.

Many schools use a unified system for indicating spelling, grammar errors, etc. If you don't have a system, you should create one.

## Self marking

This is most useful for things like maths or answers to Yes/No questions or open information questions where certain specified words or an exact answer may be expected, e.g.

---

Q – What is the square root of 16?

Q – Sont les éléphants plus grands que les souris? Oui ou Non?

Q – What was the name of Henry VIII's second wife?

Q – Comment ça va, Jean? _____ suis _____ bien, merci, Gilles.

---

You can give the answers to the class and students can self mark. You can then sit at your desk and ask students in turn for their score and enter it directly into your mark book. Your final job is then to check the books (quickly taking a note of any deviation from the learning outcomes) and initial the pages. You can do this at your leisure (!) while they are busy on a task later in the lesson. At this time you can also offer a helpful word or two increasing your personal contact a little.

## Peer marking

Almost identical except that students do not mark their own books, but swap with a neighbour and then return them after the marking is completed.

In both the above cases, you still need to collect books regularly and monitor other aspects of the work and offer feedback. But the donkey work of tick or cross is completely eliminated. You can concentrate entirely on other matters.

## In-class-time marking

You make it a very strict rule that every book is marked in class time at least once a week. When the students are quietly busy on an extended task, you can call out individual students and mark their books while they wait by your desk side. You can monitor the class from your desk and do your marking at the same time.

The only drawback to this technique is that you are unavailable for consultation by other class members while you are doing this. The task the kids are engaged on will have to be very clearly set out with no room for misunderstanding. If your class is trained to be very quietly co-operative, this will facilitate matters immensely. Small problems can then be dealt with by peers.

There are many obvious benefits. You get some one-on-one time with each and every student at least once a week and can offer precisely targeted feedback immediately.

You also never need do any other marking unless you really want to. There is, of course, no reason why you shouldn't want to. After all, there is immense benefit in it.

## Impression marking Mk I

This is a very useful technique for marking essays or other extended writing. You first of all decide on four or five criteria. You may decide, for example on: quality of understanding, spelling, grammar, layout, handwriting.

Read the text very quickly five times, each time programming your brain to assess a particular criterion. Assign a mark, say out of five, to each one. You may decide to highlight points, but don't comment on them individually. If you need to, write the numbers very lightly in pencil as an aide-memoire, then you can rub them out easily.

You can now offer very accurate feedback on five major criteria very quickly. You only need write two or three sentences.

Tarquin will spend five minutes in class understanding exactly what your note refers to. He will then write a reply underneath. He will thank you for your guidance and will explain what steps he will take to build on his strengths and eliminate his weaknesses. A little personal touch will strengthen the technique even more.

By checking Tarquin's reply, both you and he can identify with absolute precision if he had made mistakes or errors.

◆ If he made a mistake, he can self-correct.

◆ If he made an error, he needs more or remedial learning.

This last point is vital. You have spent five minutes marking Tarquin's book. Tarquin has spent five minutes in deep reflection on your extremely accurate and perceptive feedback. That is equitable and educationally excellent. It is axiomatic in Accelerated

Learning that reflection is a vital part of the learning to learn process.

## Impression Marking Mk II

This is identical except that you highlight notable points and draw a little grid, both in soft pencil.

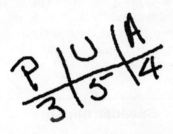

The grid here would indicate P = presentation, U = evidence of understanding, A = accuracy. In this case the child is asked to write the comments for himself using the cues that you give him. The child is looking at his work through his eyes, but also needs to understand how you look at it through your eyes. He is learning critical thinking from another person's perspective.

If he learns that and nothing else beyond basic skills in his school career, he will have learnt enough to leave school and become a multi-millionaire before he's twenty-five. (He might even donate some of his money to your school!)

This technique is educationally sound, probably the soundest of them all, and takes you seconds rather than minutes.

The same observations about mistakes and errors apply.

You can very easily mark a set of thirty books in twenty minutes or less (when you're in a flow state) AND generate far more educational benefit for Tarquin.

I wouldn't suggest that any teacher should use one method exclusively. Rather, a range of techniques should be used depending upon how much time is available, the perceived educational value of each at a particular stage and just to add variety to the children's experience.

## Speeder uppers

No matter what method of marking you use, there are certain things you must do to speed up the process.

◆ You must have a clean and tidy working space. Clear away any clutter so you can spread out your books or folders, mark book, pencil case and maybe have room for a cup of something hot to sip at every so often.

◆ You must prepare yourself to get into the flow state. You will work much faster and cut your time dramatically.

These two steps alone can cut the time spent marking by half.

◆ Marking must be done at a single sitting while in a flow state. It must be a well-understood law in the school (and at home, if marking is done there) that you must NEVER be disturbed when you are marking for anything less than armed insurrection, invasion by a foreign power, earthquake, flood or fire.

## Review

- Value marking as an outstandingly useful feed-back mechanism for everyone: you; Tarquin, Tarquin's mum, and the boss.

- Use a variety of appropriate methods of marking.

- Differentiate between mistakes and errors.

- Prepare your workspace.

- Prepare your equipment.

- Prepare yourself to get into the flow state.

- Prepare to repel all boarders.

- Start.

- Don't stop until you have finished.

- Make sure that the students get the feedback you give them. Set them an exercise to reply or make some other note to show that they have benefited from your investment.

## 6

# Report Writing

- Context
- Why write reports?
- What goes into a report?
- Preparing information
- Report-writing software
- Preparing a template
- Preparing the comments
- Review

## Context

The school report is an accurate and concise summary of a student's performance in a variety of areas. Report writing should be an excellent use of your time.

It should be effective in that the report fulfils its purpose of being a clear and meaningful assessment of a student's strengths and weaknesses and a source of guidance. Everybody should benefit by its existence.

It should be efficient in that you can write excellent reports in the shortest possible time.

# Why write reports?

Report writing is important for a variety of reasons and purposes. Remember that you must be able to focus on the benefits! That's the first secret.

## *For the school*

It is important to have a permanent record and point of reference in case any enquiries about a student are made at any time. The accuracy and care taken over the reports are an indication of the school's commitment to the students. They also indicate to the school any remedial action which may need to be taken.

## *For you*

Reports are a constant reminder of what the most important issue is: the education of children. It is sometimes all too easy to lose sight of the fact that schools actually exist first and foremost to help our children develop the knowledge, understanding and skills that they will find helpful as they approach and reach adulthood.

## *For parents*

The school report is a wonderful opportunity to encourage parents/caregivers to take an active interest in their children's schooling. It gives guidance on how the parent can help the child to take advantage of the education they are receiving. It acts as a reassurance that their child is being treated as an individual and that individual needs and wants are being addressed.

## *For the student*

The report gives a summary of performance and should give a very clear indication of how progress can be maintained and/or improved.

Take a clean page in your notebook and concept map this. The more reasons you can come up with, the more committed you will be to making an excellent job of your report writing and the more benefit you will see in it.

# What goes into a report?

A report must contain information about many areas of a student's school life.

At the very minimum it should contain an assessment of academic performance and helpful advice and comments.

At the other extreme it may be a complete analysis of everything academic, inter-personal, intra-personal and developmental.

Create your mental picture of your reports by considering the kind of information that you need to include. This will depend on your roles. A reception class teacher will have one set of criteria and a head of sixth form will have a very different set.

Do your thinking first, but get it down onto paper. Make a concept shower of the different criteria that you need to consider when you come to write the reports.

## Preparing information

While you can use your mark book for this, I recommend that you keep a separate notebook. It does take a little extra time to prepare, but the time will be repaid later come report-writing time.

Make a class list as shown below. In the spaces on the top row you will record the different criteria that you want to comment on. It's a good idea to leave a few blank boxes to the right as you will probably want to add criteria as the year progresses.

Keep the criteria in groups. You may want a group of criteria describing academic progress, another one for behavioural issues, etc. This type of grouping helps you differentiate and focus on different aspects of the students' personalities and performances.

This notebook is left open on your desk every lesson.

| | Timekeeping | Participation | Neatness | Accuracy | Effort | Enthusiasm | Organization | |
|---|---|---|---|---|---|---|---|---|
| Arbuthnot Artless | | | | | | | | |
| Bettie Bloomer | | | | | | | | |
| Caruthers Clott | | | | | | | | |
| Damien Doppler | | | | | | | | |
| | | | | | | | | |

## Every Minute Counts

As you notice a child's particular strength or weakness in any of the criteria you can simply put a + (for a strength) or a − (for a weakness). If you wish to record a particular strength or weakness you can double the signs.

Of course, you may find that you get pluses and minuses in the same boxes throughout the year! Not every student performs at the same level every day. This in itself is a valuable thing to record.

In some lessons you may decide to take an in-depth look at a particular criterion for the entire class. You are then able to make up a very accurate profile of the entire class in that area!

In other lessons you may decide to concentrate on one particular child and build up a very accurate profile across the whole range of criteria.

You may want to add more information to this while you have their exercise books in for marking.

You can see straightaway how this form of record keeping allows you to do several things:

- You can focus very precisely on the important strengths and weaknesses.

- You can build up a very accurate class profile which will almost certainly affect the way you teach.

- You can build up a very accurate profile for each individual student which will help you identify any issues of concern.

- You can take remedial action when it becomes evident that it is needed.

- You can do it all in almost no time at all.

## Report-writing software

Some schools use software packages with standardized formats and comment banks. These are great time savers (provided you have done the preparation outlined above). The problem is that the final reports tend to be bland and lifeless, and parents do notice this.

Of course, having used a software package to save time, you don't then want to spend more time re-writing the entire report to make it look like it was written by a real person. If anything, this will take more time than writing the report in the first place.

If you don't have this facility, you can prepare your own hand-written system.

## Preparing a template

You must have a pre-designed template for any comments that you are going to write. This could be provided by the school or your department. If it isn't, you should prepare a template for yourself and have it approved by your line manager.

The question is, 'How do I come up with a template?'

There are 5 steps.

1. Put yourself in the position of a parent. Make a concept shower of all the information that a parent would want from your report.

2. Put yourself back in your position as a teacher. Make a concept shower of all the information that you want to give.

3. Take both concept showers and see where they overlap. That's the essential information to give. (Neither you nor the parent can have it all, but you can both have the essential!)

4. Spend some time and write a powerful and dynamic report for one student. This will probably take some time as you reduce it and reduce it until only the most essential information is included in a powerful and accessible way. The language must be easy to understand and points must be made clearly and concisely.

5. Turn this into a template by putting gaps where the specific information will go.

You now have the perfect template for your reports. Because it has been created by a real live human being (you) to suit your own needs and those of the parents it won't produce the sterile reports of a software package. All you need to do now is to fill in the blanks!

Naturally, there will be instances where you want to add specific information for a particular student who has highly idiosyncratic needs. You're a teacher, you're very intelligent, you can adapt anything to anything; it's not a problem.

## Preparing the comments

You can create you own comment bank and it could hardly be easier. A few pages of an exercise book or a few pages printed off on your computer with standard and easily adaptable comments which simply drop into the blanks of your template is all you need. This saves you hours. Again, you might need to clear these with your line manager.

You can see how a moderate investment of time is going to save you very many hours AND will probably improve the quality of your reports as well. And, most importantly, you have all the thinking completely done. When it comes time to write the reports they almost write themselves!

# Review

◆ Writing reports is of great benefit to all concerned.

◆ Do your thinking first, production comes second.

◆ Decide on the precise contents of the report before you start writing.

◆ Keep records of all the criteria that you want to include in your reports and that will help you come report-writing time.

◆ Prepare a template that will include all the essential information.

◆ Prepare a comments bank.

◆ As ever, prepare to get into a flow state before writing a single word.

# 7

# How to Handle Paperwork

- ◆ Context
- ◆ The system
- ◆ How it works
- ◆ Benefits of the system
- ◆ Review

## Context

You get a terrific amount of paperwork to deal with, so a foolproof system is needed.

## The system

You need FOUR pocket folders labelled: IN, TODAY, LATER, DONE.

You want pocket folders rather than trays because they are portable in your briefcase and it's much easier to see what's in there. My experience of trays is that they get cluttered up with all sorts of rubbish. Yours may be different.

**IN**: Every time a new piece of paper appears, it goes

into this folder straightaway – except those that can simply be passed on immediately.

**TODAY**: Pretty obviously, this is for all the papers that you are going to deal with today.

**LATER**: Again, what goes in here is pretty obvious. This folder is for jobs that can safely be left.

**DONE**: Every piece of paper that has been dealt with goes in this folder. Once the paperwork is finished, the contents of this folder can be actioned as appropriate: filed, delivered, passed on or whatever.

## How it works

Every morning check your mailbox and check everything very quickly. If there is anything that can be done immediately, do it. (For example, pass a paper on to someone else.) Everything else goes straight into the IN folder.

When you get back to your desk, empty the IN folder and anything in the LATER folder onto your desk. Go through the papers and distribute them into the TODAY folder for things to be attended to today (taking account of how much time you are going to dedicate to paperwork) and the LATER folder for things that can wait.

You have already planned time during the day to deal with paperwork. Before you start, take the time to relax and get yourself ready for the flow state. Empty the TODAY folder onto your desk top and sort the papers out into the order that you want to deal with them.

Different people have different approaches. Some like to get the quickies out of the way and then work on the complex, others vice versa. Try both ways on alternate days until you find which is better for you. You may find that you prefer to mix them up into types.

It really doesn't matter which you choose, but it does help to have some kind of system. If you work with a system that appeals to your particular working style and to your energy profile, you will naturally be more effective and efficient.

As each paper is finished, put it into the DONE folder immediately. You won't lose it and it won't clutter up your desk or your vision.

The last thing to do is to deal with the DONE folder. Distribute the papers as necessary.

If, as so often happens, a paper is delivered during the day, it can be put into either the IN folder (if it is not urgent) or the TODAY folder (if it is). You probably won't put it into the LATER folder because that will be out of sight in a drawer or, better, in your briefcase.

A word of advice: if someone is hassling you for a paper and the urgency isn't of your own making, ask them to come and see you at a time that suits you. Make sure that it is completed and give it to them when they come. If you do this a few times they will get the message.

Whatever you do, don't get up in the middle of a paperwork session and go playing postman. This will destroy your flow and slow you down to half speed or less.

## Benefits of the system

As long as you follow the system, it is absolutely foolproof.

◆ Nothing can get lost.

◆ Nothing can get passed over.

◆ Nothing can get mislaid.

◆ You get the jobs done earlier rather than later.

◆ You cannot possibly miss a deadline.

◆ You get into flow state working.

I'm often asked what is wrong with the three-tray (IN, OUT, PENDING) system. The answer is that there's nothing wrong with it, as long as it's used wisely. I developed the four-folder system simply because it is utterly foolproof (and I'm a fool) and portable. I can carry the folders in my briefcase. If I get an odd few minutes of otherwise dead time, I can delve into my TODAY folder and get a few Q jobs done and then put them straight into the DONE folder.

Again, you may want to apply the 3 As to it and adapt it to your own preferred working style.

## Review

◆ Sort papers into one of your two working files as early as possible.

◆ Assign a definite time that you will spend on paperwork.

## Every Minute Counts

- Prepare your working space and have everything ready to hand.

- Start approaching the flow state before you start on the paperwork.

- If someone is hassling you for a paper and it's not your problem, get them to come to you if it saves you time.

- Do not allow any interruptions while you are doing your paperwork.

- When each paper is dealt with transfer it to your DONE folder.

- The final job is to distribute the completed tasks from the DONE folder.

**8**

# How to Run Meetings

- Context
- Why hold meetings?
- Why you need this
- Roles
- General notes
- Review

## Context

Meetings are the bane of everybody's life. They very seldom achieve much of what they set out to achieve. Eyes roll to the heavens at the mention of them and the deep sighs can be sensed if not heard.

It doesn't have to be this way. Meetings can be, indeed MUST be, an excellent use of your time.

## Why hold meetings?

I suspect that many have asked this question before me and not found a good reason. You actually need a good reason – remember the first secret of time! It applies to meetings just as much as to anything else.

Meetings actually fulfil many useful purposes:

◆ Transfer of information

◆ Problem-solving

◆ Decision-making

◆ Democratizing

◆ Wisdom-collecting

◆ Opinion-sounding/sharing

◆ Buy in

etc.

There's nothing wrong with meetings. It's the way that they are run that is the problem! That need not be the case if a few simple rules and procedures are followed.

## Why you need this

In order for meetings to have a useful role they need to be well run and effective. It's worth repeating that good time management means being effective and efficient. If meetings are to fulfil these two criteria they must be well run.

## Roles

If you are calling a meeting:

◆ First of all ask yourself if there really is a need. If you are only holding a meeting because it is a school or departmental tradition and there is nothing essential, consider scrapping it.

- You must circulate an agenda in advance of the meeting. It need not be a long document, indeed, the shorter the better. Don't forget to put the location! Add a note that if any of the attendees have any points to add, they must inform you ASAP before the meeting. This is to allow you time to decide how and if they will be included. Put the names of all the attendees at the top. This helps you to deliver to all the necessary people (tick a name on each copy and deliver it to their pigeon hole or hand). It also lets the attendees know who else is attending and maybe they can have some preliminary discussion.

- Circulate it at least two days before the meeting.

- Book the room.

  If you are chairing a meeting:

- You are responsible for the smooth running of the meeting, so run it smoothly. The meeting can only be productive if the chair is effective.

- Start the meeting on time. If anyone is late, it is their problem and not that of those who are on time. Do not recap for their benefit unless it is absolutely vital. If it is, first of all apologize to the others for wasting their time.

- Start by going over the agenda, explaining how much time will be assigned to each item and exactly what the expected outcomes are.

# Every Minute Counts

The ground is now prepared for a productive meeting. Everyone has a very clear idea about what is going to happen, how long it should take and exactly what the expected outcomes are. One issue which may take more time than anticipated is taken care of already. The promise has been made that if it takes longer than a few minutes, another meeting of interested parties only will be arranged.

When contentious or otherwise debatable points are on the table, a simple system should be used.

1. Presentation of facts and facts only. Opinions and emotions are not to be brought up at this stage. Facts should be noted on a whiteboard or flip chart. This separates the fact from the person who brought it up – always a good idea.

2. Positive suggestions and ideas only. At this stage opinions and emotions can be brought in to the discussion. It is important to be very strict about the positive aspects at this stage. No argument or disagreements must be allowed.

3. Negative suggestions and ideas only. The same rules apply as for 2.

4. Open discussion. The chair must be very strict here and not allow:

   - domination by one or two individuals
   - repetition (Cut it short immediately. A good way of doing this is by cutting in and paraphrasing. Then say, 'I think we all understand that now!')
   - mini-meetings or discussion groups
   - new facts being brought in

Everyone who wants to speak must be allowed to. A raised hand should be respected and the person invited to contribute. Anyone who is not contributing much should be invited to make their input. (They frequently have the best ideas.)

Do not allow senior promoted staff to bully. They are subject to your authority while you are in the chair.

The discussion must be driven forwards and onwards towards a conclusion.

5. A clear and unequivocal statement of the final decision.

   - Bring the meeting to a close by giving a brief synopsis of the decisions arrived at, what further action will be taken and by whom and when.

[If you really want to get into this, get a copy of *Six Thinking Hats* by de Bono. See Reading List.]

- If any points are purely informational, they should be accompanied by notes. You cannot expect people at a meeting to spend all their time scribbling down notes from very dense information. That is a complete waste of time. The notes should be circulated beforehand. If the information is not that important, but falls in the 'useful but not essential to know' category, it would better be put on the school's Intranet and a reference given.

If you are attending a meeting:

- Ask yourself if you really need to be there. Being there to make up numbers isn't a good reason. If you don't need to be there, consider asking to be excused.

- If you have anything that needs to be addressed in the meeting but is not on the agenda, tell the convenor in plenty of time. There is then time for the convenor to plan if and how it can be fitted in to the meeting.

- Take your logbook with you and aim to keep the briefest of notes. It's useful to take/make notes in soft pencil and then go over them in ink later while the information is still fresh in your mind. Rub out the pencil notes.

- As an alternative, keep your meeting notes on A4 and keep them in a dedicated file or a section of your staff file.

- Keep yourself involved. Don't get into mini-meetings on the side.

- Behave yourself. Don't drop bombshells or rise to others who do.

   If you are calling a briefing:

- Ask yourself if it is really necessary for other people. If it isn't, don't call it.

- Use an excellent outline system:

   *Overview* – Say what the briefing is about.
   *Preview* – Give the main points that will be covered. Write them on a board or flip chart high on the left-hand side.
   *Inview* – Use a clean flip chart page for each major point and use bullets for minor points.
   *Review* – Refer again to the preview and summarize what you have talked about.

- Put a summary on the school's Intranet.

(In the case of the boss's morning briefing, if the agenda cannot be circulated in advance, it can be put on a flip chart page and blu-tacked to a wall. Similarly, put a copy on the Intranet.)

## General notes

- Whatever you do or do not do in a meeting, don't drop bombshells.

- High horses are best left at home or tethered up elsewhere.

- Facts count.

- Opinions are like precious metals: their value increases with rarity and desirability. Other people are always a better judge of the overall value of your opinions than you are!

## Review

- Only hold meetings that are absolutely essential.

- Only attend meetings that are absolutely essential.

- No matter what your role, prepare for meetings beforehand.

- There must be an agenda.

- Always discuss facts, the upsides of an issue and then the downsides of an issue in that order before coming to any decisions.

- Manners matter.

**Part Three**

# Quick Tips

## Your briefcase

Some years ago I had to scrap an old car. I took it to the junk yard and negotiated a reasonable price. The owner took me into his office to finalize the details and the paperwork. It was exactly the kind of office that you would expect in a junk yard – full of junk.

He then took out his briefcase and opened it on his knee. He had everything that he needed and nothing that he didn't need. It was the neatest briefcase I'd ever seen.

When I expressed my admiration for his case he was a little taken aback. 'How do you expect me to run a business without an office?' he asked me. 'This is my office,' he said, pointing to his case.

Ever since that day I have been a convert to the merits of a well-organized briefcase.

You should be too.

Make a list of all the jobs that you need to do, all the papers to which you need instant access at any time and all the materials that you need to do the job.

This includes pens, pencils, erasers, pencil sharpeners, stapler, staple remover, calculator, rubber stamps, note pad, your diary and logbook, incident reports and all the other paraphernalia. Carry them in your briefcase and have your case with you at all times. You are then primed and ready for action.

One thing you must certainly keep in your case is a block of post-it notes or similar. They are invaluable for taking messages or leaving brief notes, adding notes to documents that you pass on, etc. You can even use them to send yourself messages!

Avoid carrying things that you really don't need. Spring clean your case every week or so and get rid of excess bits of paper, old newspapers, etc. You need to avoid clutter in your briefcase as much as anywhere else.

If you've got a top-opening case, you'd probably be better off getting a new one with an opening lid. They really are much easier to use as they already have pockets fitted and spaces for your different bits and pieces.

You might also want to consider having two briefcases. One is for work and the other for other everyday living business.

## Clutter

You've heard of feng shui – the Chinese art of housekeeping. Some people are making a very good living out of helping others get rid of clutter in their lives. Yes, that's basically what feng shui is all about. It's about living and working in a pleasant and stimulating environment. There may well be something in the ideas of energy flow and orientation, I cannot say for sure. But I CAN say that living without clutter is much happier and more productive than the alternatives.

Staffroom, workroom, departmental office, stock cupboard. They all have to be kept free of clutter. Research has shown that the average office worker spends upwards of an hour a day (in 2 and 3-minute periods) searching for things like pens, rulers, bits of paper, etc. I don't know of any research done with teachers, but I would be surprised if it was very much less than twenty minutes a day. The prime culprit is clutter.

There is only one answer: don't allow any clutter anywhere for any reason. You really do have to be utterly ruthless.

*Your desk*: This is your mission control centre. Keep it like one. (Can you imagine it? 'Houston. We have a problem.' 'Hang on a minute, I'll just go and get a pen. Yes, I've got one here. No, wait. It's empty. I'll just go next door and get another one.')

*Magazines*: Sort them out. Cut out and file interesting articles. Put a piece of A4 at the front of the file and put a brief description of the articles. Ditch the rest.

*Newspapers*: The same as magazines. Cut out the interesting bits of *TES*, *Grauniad*, etc. and ditch the rest.

*Random papers*: After due notice (1 day is quite sufficient) sweep any papers lying about in any public areas into a very large cardboard box. If anyone has a paper they really need they can search through a cardboard box. After two or three days, empty the box into a skip.

*Work tables*: At the end of every working day, sweep any papers, books, pens, pencils, etc. into a large cardboard box. If Mr Curdleblood can't find the papers he left there yesterday, it's his problem. He can search the box for them. The one thing Mr Curdleblood must not be permitted to do is allow his untidiness to slow down other people.

*Offices*: If you're going to keep it, file it. If you're going to file it, make sure that the files are clearly marked and stored properly on shelves and not piled up on the floor. If you're not going to file it, chuck it. Throw away last year's catalogue as soon as this year's comes in.

*Resource rooms*: File everything, store everything and label everything. It is utterly pointless having resources if no one knows where anything is or cannot find it because it's underneath a pile of other stuff.

*Filing cabinets*: Consider throwing the hanging files away and replacing them with expandable pocket files. Hanging files take up vast amounts of room even when empty. The expandable pocket files can be removed more easily and the contents sorted more easily. Label them with sticky labels so they can be re-labelled easily some other time.

Make your filing categories fairly broad. You don't want to have a file with just one paper in it. On the other hand, you don't want to have the file too heavy to pull out without it ripping. Intelligence is called for.

*Book shelves*: Keep them tidy and full of current books. Put just a few of the frequently used books on the 'useful books' shelf and all the others on another shelf. If a book from either shelf is used and found useful, replace it among the 'useful books'. The 'useful books' shelf will grow with time and the other shelf will diminish. After 12 months, get rid of most of the books which remain on the other shelf. Only keep those which have a very good chance of making it to keep company with the other 'useful' books.

This system is organic as the contents of the 'useful' shelf grows to an optimum size. Evolution at its best.

*Old equipment*: It's time to get rid of the Gestetner and the Banda machine. Old dot-matrix printers, calculators with broken displays ... get rid of them!

Clear all the clutter out of your school, out of your briefcase, handbag, out of your car, house, garage, garden ... all the places where clutter can accumulate. Spring clean everything and everywhere.

You'll be amazed at just how much better you feel living in an environment that is clean and bright and completely clutter-free.

## Communication skills

Good communication skills will help you be much more effective and efficient. They will help you do the right thing at the right time and give and get the information quickly and effectively. It is well known that poor communication is responsible for many relationship breakdowns and huge amounts of time and effort being wasted. Resolve never to be the victim of this particular problem.

### Reading

There are two very effective approaches that will save you time and make your reading better.

(i) *SQ3R* – Skim, Question, Read, Recite, Review.

(ii) *4-Views* – Overview, Preview, Inview, Review.

They both work on the same basic principle: you grasp the information better if you build it up bit-by-bit.

They both work very well.

## *Writing*

The key to effective writing is to put yourself in the reader's shoes. Don't worry about what information you want to give. Concern yourself with the information that the reader wants to get.

As with every endeavour, planning time is repaid very many times over.

What are the key words and key ideas that the reader needs? Plan them using either a concept shower or a concept map. Allow yourself to make as many associations as possible and let your mind run free. Once you have done this, you can start to order the ideas into the shortest and most powerful form possible.

When you start writing, do just that. Start writing and don't stop. Just let the words flow onto the page and allow yourself to wax as lyrical as possible. Don't worry about form or style or even spelling. Whatever you do, don't stop and edit. That will just ruin the flow and slow you down.

After a while, come back and edit ONCE as carefully as possible. At this stage you are looking to cut out redundancy and increase the power and flow.

If it is possible, you may like to get an independent

third party to check it over. Please listen to what they say. A second and final edit should finish the job.

## Speaking

When you have to give information it's a good idea to use a three or four-step approach. I prefer a four-step.

- Overview
- Preview
- Inview
- Review

Naturally, it's a conversation so you can't prepare a speech, but you can clarify in your mind exactly what the important points are. If you don't do this, how is your listener going to get a clear idea?

A conversation might go something like this:

*You*: Jenny. Could we have a quick word about the arrangements for ... on ...? (Overview)
*Jenny*: Yes, of course.
*You*: There are two main points. First of all there's ... And we also need to discuss ... (Preview)

The conversation now continues (Inview)
And finally ...

*You*: So that's OK, is it? You'll ... and I'll ... And you'll let your class know tomorrow morning. (Review)
*Jenny*: Yes, that's fine.

And information is transmitted quickly and effectively.

## Listening

Everybody thinks they are above-average listeners. Everybody thinks they are above-average drivers. At least half are wrong. For safety's sake, it is always better to assume that you are below-average and take extra care.

Most people don't actually listen for anything other than a gap in the other person's monologue so they can re-launch into theirs. This doesn't lead to good dialogue. (It is frequently referred to as the dialogue of the deaf.)

There is a very simple formula for being a good listener: S A I L

- S = shut up

- A = ask questions

- I = involve yourself

- L = look at the speaker

*Shut up* means exactly that. Most conversations are not dialogues, they are co-synchronous monologues. You need to listen to the information being given, and you can't speak at the same time.

*Ask questions*. Ask the speaker questions and ask yourself questions at the same time. You can think about twelve times as fast as anyone can speak. Take advantage of this and hold an internal dialogue at the same time.

*Involve yourself* and commit to the conversation. It can only be to your benefit to get the information, so pay attention to it. Be attend-minded. Involve yourself with the speaker and empathize. This will make it much easier for the speaker to open up to you.

Let your body language show that you are involved and interject frequently with positive cues. If the speaker drifts off onto a tangent, you can bring them back if you are involved. If you aren't, you are a slave to the direction that the speaker takes you.

*Look at the speaker*. It is estimated that between 65 per cent and 92 per cent of information is transmitted non-verbally. You will miss this completely if you don't look. You also get visual cues to hang the aural cues on which makes it much easier to remember what was said and the context in which it was said.

## Planning your day

There is a lot of debate these days about the work–life balance. It isn't very helpful because the terminology is misleading. There is no balance between work and life because work is such a big part of life. The correct term is life balance.

Your job then is to design your day to get the correct balance.

The easiest way is to plan your day in three parts. Beginning, middle and end.

Most of this book is concerned with the middle bit – the time you spend at work and making it as productive as possible. The way to do that is to commit to spending 40 high-productivity hours at work and 40 hours on other aspects of living away from work.

## Start the day well

You want to wake up in the morning refreshed after a good night's sleep and in plenty of time so you aren't rushing around. Have a bath or a shower and pamper yourself a little. Do a bit of bending and stretching to loosen up your body and mind ready for the rigours of the day. Maybe go for a brisk walk and pick up a newspaper if you have a shop handy.

A good healthy breakfast will ensure that you have enough energy to get through the day until lunch time. Make sure that breakfast is a well-balanced meal; have some cereals, orange juice, toast, a boiled egg or omelette and a piece of fruit. Eat your breakfast without TV. Rather spend the time chatting with the family and talking about your hopes for this bright new day you have been granted.

Leave home in plenty of time so you aren't going to arrive at work in a state of exhaustion. Spend a minute or two sitting in the car before going into school. Use this time to reflect and calm yourself before the onslaught.

## End the day well

When you get home in the evening, you are going home for a purpose. That purpose is to live a full and happy life with your family. Again, it might help to sit in the car for a moment or two and take stock before going inside.

When you get home, take some time to re-connect with the family and get back onto their wavelength. Ask about their day and what they have achieved. Tell them the funny things that have happened to you. (Whatever you do, don't moan. Leave all the stresses and strains of the job at school where they belong. You want to set the tone for a pleasant family time and moaning isn't going to do that!)

Have a family meal at the table without the TV. Any meal can be incredibly enhanced with the simple addition of a couple of candles and the subtraction of the TV.

During the evening, make sure that you spend some time on self care. You need to keep yourself well serviced, just like the car. Service your mind and do some good reading. Service your body and get some appropriate exercise. Both will serve you better if they are well exercised and in tip-top condition. They will only be that way if you take care of them.

Some people find it a good idea to set an alarm clock for getting ready for sleep.

It is always a good idea to slow down over a period of about 30 minutes before going to bed. Do a little yoga or some bending and stretching and a few rounds of deep breathing to limber up your body and calm the mind. Maybe read a little or write a few lines in a reflective journal. Focus on the good parts of the day and the wonderful lessons you have learned.

Don't drink tea or coffee in the two hours before bed. They will prevent you from getting to sleep quickly. Similarly, don't do any strenuous exercise just before bedtime.

A shower or bath can be very relaxing and then climb into a nice warm comfortable bed ready to drop off into a deep and restful sleep ready to start again, awakening refreshed in the morning.

(The slowing-down process is very important to good restful sleep. Have you ever noticed how traditional children's bedtime stories are constructed? They are very well designed to do just this.)

## Your memory

Even with the best Master List and To Do list system in the world, you need to remember things. I never cease to be amazed at the number of people who say, almost with pride in their voices, 'Oh, I've got a memory like a sieve.' They don't actually mean that they have a poor memory. What they mean is that they are absent-minded.

The way to overcome being absent-minded is obvious. Simply be the opposite. Be ATTEND-MINDED.

Yes, it really is as simple as that.

Absent-mindedness is not the same as forgetting, it is not registering the information in the first place.

As soon as someone asks you to do something or pass on a message or whatever, FIX IT in your memory by focusing your mind on the message. Pay attention to exactly what it is that you need to do and repeat it to yourself.

Here's an example: you're on your way to class and Mr Curdleblood asks you to remind Tarquin to bring his money for a new clarinet reed to the music room. How do you make sure that you remember it?

Focus your attention on Mr Curdleblood. Smile at him and repeat what he asked you to do. 'OK. I'll ask him straightaway,' you say and then get a mental picture of Tarquin playing his clarinet with £ signs coming out of it instead of musical notes. It's fixed and you won't forget it.

Simply being attend-minded will overcome any tendency to be absent-minded.

When you put your car keys down somewhere, simply tell yourself, 'I've put the car keys on the window ledge, between the plant and that awful vase Auntie Gertie gave us.' Glance at the place for a moment and fix it in your memory. You'll find your keys when you need them.

There is a popular myth that one's memory inevitably deteriorates with age. This is utterly untrue. As long as your brain is healthy and you are not suffering from any degenerative disorder, your memory can be excellent well into old age. What is true is that your 'memory muscles' get flabby and ineffective if you don't make a conscious effort to keep them in good order. (Your stomach muscles go the same way, as you may have noticed!)

There are lots of things you can do to improve your memory and all of them will save you time and make you more effective and efficient.

## Relaxation

I don't only train teachers how to manage time, I also do stress-management training. Teaching is the most stressful of all professions for a variety of reasons. One of them is that we are 'on-show' for three hours at a time with only a few minutes' break between classes.

It's even worse for primary school staff, particularly if there is a wet break!

It's vital to relax at every opportunity. If you can simply let go for as little as five minutes, you will make yourself much more resilient and able to cope with the stress of the next class. If you don't take these opportunities, you are really asking for trouble.

Make sure that you build time into your lessons for you to get a few minutes' peace and quiet. Give the kids at least five minutes on a silent activity every lesson. Apart from focusing their attention, it gives you a few minutes to just sit and watch them.

Don't go rushing around at break times delivering messages and collecting books, etc. It's counter-productive. Make sure that you do all these things at other times when you have the time to do them. (Good planning makes you able to do this.)

Each break time, sit down, maybe with a hot drink, and really chill out. Practise a few rounds of slow, deep belly breathing. Close your eyes and go on a two-minute mental holiday.

You must have a relaxing lunch break. It has been proven over and over again that you will be very much more productive in the afternoon if you have a decent break at midday. It's a good idea to go for a little walk to get your energy levels and oxygen levels up for a while. This will stimulate your mental muscles as well as your body's muscles.

Have another short break after school finishes before you start on your other work. Again, you will be much more productive if you re-vitalize yourself.

Remember, no one cares how much time you put in. The only thing that counts is results. You will produce very much better results in much less time if you take the time to ensure that you are working at peak efficiency. That means that you work in a relaxed and aware state.

# Reading List

## *Time management*

Covey, Stephen R. (1999) *First Things First*, Simon & Schuster.
Mayer, Jeffrey L. (1999) *Time Management for Dummies*, IDG Books.

## *The flow state*

Stine, Jean Marie (1997) *Double Your Brainpower*, Prentice Hall.
Wilson, Paul (2000) *Calm For Life*, Penguin.

## *Mission statements*

Covey, Stephen R. (1999) *The 7 Habits of Highly Effective People*, Simon & Schuster.

## *Thinking and problem-solving*

Bono, Edward de (2000) *Six Thinking Hats*, Penguin Books.
Bono, Edward de (1993) *Teach Your Child How To Think*, Penguin.
Bono, Edward de (1996) *Teach Yourself To Think*, Penguin.

# Reading List

## Memory

Buzan, Tony (2003) *Use Your Memory*, BBC Books.
Kurland, Michael and Lupoff, Richard (1999) *The Complete Idiot's Guide To Improving Your Memory*, Alpha Books.

## Concept mapping

Buzan, Tony (2003) *Use Your Head*, BBC Books.
Buzan, Tony and Barry (2000) *The Mind Map Book*, BBC Books.

## Positive Mental Attitude (PMA)

Peale, Norman Vincent (1998) *The Power of Positive Thinking*, Cedar Books.
Sartwell, Matthew (ed.) (1999) *Napoleon Hill's Keys to Success*, Plume Books.

## Goal setting

Robbins, Anthony (1992) *Awaken the Giant Within*, Simon & Schuster.

## The 'Black Box'

Assessment Reform Group (2002) *Assessment for Learning: Beyond the Black Box*, *http://www.assessment-reform-group.org.uk/AssessInsides.pdf*
Black, Paul and Wiliam, Dylan (2001) *Inside the Black Box: Raising Standards through Classroom Assessment*, King's College, London, *http://www.kcl.ac.uk/depsta/education/publications/Black%20Box.pdf*